FIRST EDITION
of

A Guide to
Responsible
UNDERSEA
Exploration

A Guide to
Responsible
UNDERSEA
Exploration

CAPTAIN DOMINIC ADDARIO

Adventure in Discovery
Publisher of Adventure Books
JUPITER - FLORIDA

Adventure in Discovery Publishing
2010 FIRST EDITION

Publisher: Adventure in Discovery www.adventureindiscovery.com

ISBN: 978-0-9743414-2-2

Library of Congress Control Number: 2010905364
Printed in the United States of America

Photo credits: Cover - Punchstock.com, Aerial photography on page 10 - Paul Herrick, Shutterstock.com page 14. All other illustrations and photos from the Dominic A.Addario personal library.

NOTICE

A Guide to Responsible Undersea Exploration was written to help educate divers who may happen upon what they believe to be undiscovered treasure or artifacts. This book is approved to be used as a manual for a PADI Distinctive Specialty Course. It is important to understand that there may be jurisdictional laws and issues that are in direct contradiction to the steps or processes discussed in this book. If you decide on your own to proceed, you may be breaking a law and subject to major penalties or even incarceration. It is the reader's responsibility to research the *site specific laws* governing such discoveries and then decide for themselves whether they wish to follow any of the steps and processes discussed in *A Guide to Responsible Undersea Exploration*.

AUTHOR'S NOTE:

My wife, Yvonne, has authored and published a book for young adults entitled, *Treasure Diving with Captain Dom*. It can be ordered nationally through Barnes & Noble, Borders and other fine bookstores and retail outlets. Her primary goals were to stimulate the interest of young adults in undersea exploration while setting the record straight concerning our ongoing exploration of the Jupiter (Fla.) Historic Shipwreck Site.

Treasure Diving with Captain Dom is featured in bookstores in the young adults, local interest or "juvenile" sections. It is jammed with color photos illustrating Yvonne's explanations of how to become a young undersea explorer.

My goal in authoring *A Guide to Responsible Undersea Exploration (RUE)* is to put together an adult version of her fine work. *RUE* is for anyone interested in snorkeling, SCUBA diving and the world it opens to all who participate in this ever-growing pastime. This book is based on my practical experiences over two decades of underwater exploration and discovery. Use it as a "primer" as you embark on your own adventures.

Please enjoy this work and the spirit of its intentions.

Sincerely,
Captain Dominic A. Addario

For those Master Divers or Educational Instructing Institutes wishing to teach a PADI approved Distinctive Specialty Diver Training Course, questions and answer pamphlets are available at www.jupitercoins.com.

MRV Enterprise over the
Jupiter Historic Shipwreck

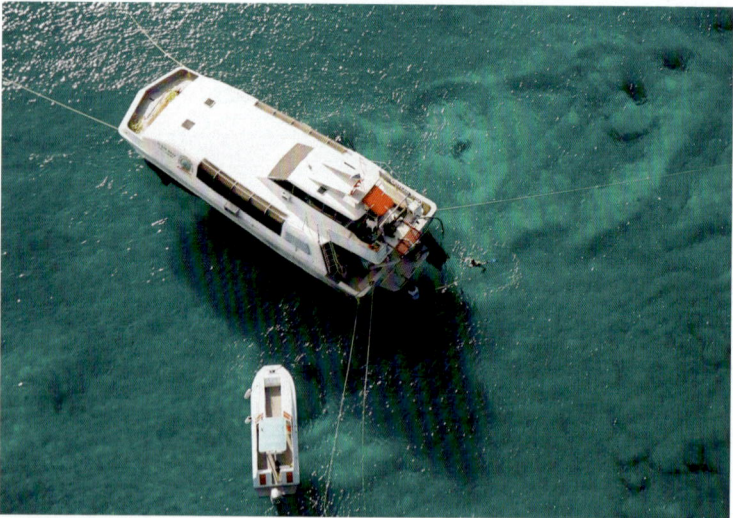

Diving over the Jupiter Historic Shipwreck Site
in only 10 feet of water

Foreword

A fascinating world of undersea exploration opens up to all of us who train in SCUBA.

As the undersea world becomes increasingly more accessible to all who take the steps of becoming well-trained SCUBA divers, a responsibility comes to better understand this barely explored frontier.

Sea levels rise and fall over the millennia due to ice ages, natural catastrophes such as meteor impacts and volcanic eruptions, and only God or the devil may know what else. This causes our oceans to resemble gigantic natural recycling facilities. The process has been going on for billions of years. It now appears plausible that mankind is accelerating global climate change, causing sea levels to rise at an even more rapid pace.

To the untrained terrestrial eye, almost everything under the sea is impacted by the saline nature of much of the water, evaporation cycles and the incompressibility of the water. In the seas, the constant rising and lowering of tides, tidal currents and wave action creates a propensity for marine life to grow quickly and obscure artifacts or man-made objects underwater. Next, add man's influence during the last two million years or so of evolution. Originally we had a propensity to wander, explore and colonize. Bodies of water and our oceans became convenient dumpsites for man's unwanted refuse. The combined effects of marine growth and time have created a situation that is ripe for observational investigations.

Modern man knows more about outer space than we know about the seven-tenths of our earth's surface that lies underwater! In fact, it's only in the last 60 or so years that the sport of SCUBA has begun to open a window of opportunity for many to spend relatively extended stretches of time underwater; thus we've been able to begin the odyssey of adventure to learn more about that which ultimately supports all life upon our "blue planet."

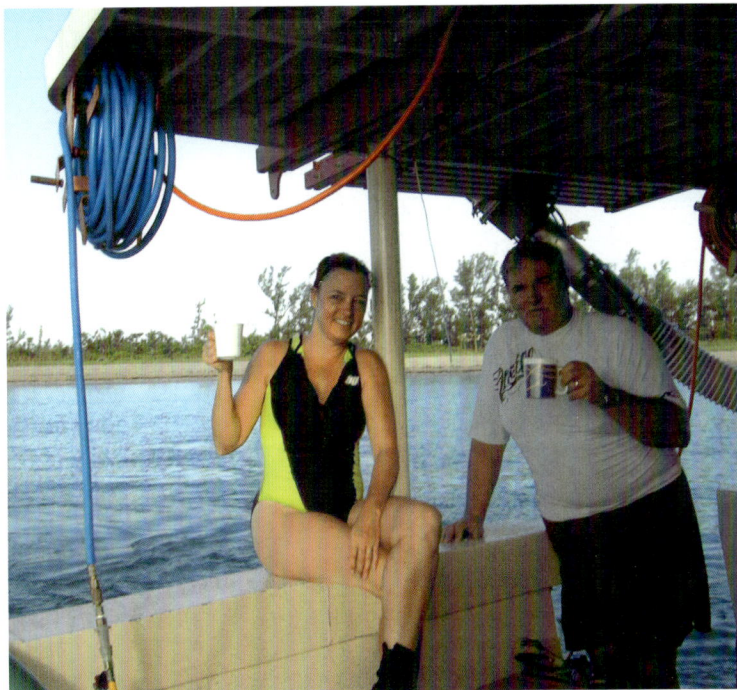

Yvonne and I on the *MRV Enterprise* at the
Jupiter Historic Shipwreck

My wife Yvonne and I encourage you to use *RUE*, its accompanying syllabus, and *Treasure Diving with Captain Dom* as learning tools for your underwater adventures in discovery as you become a responsible 21st Century Undersea SCUBA Diving Explorer.

Woman diving over wreck (Thistlegorm Red Sea)

Contents

Introduction 15

Equipment Needs 29

Site Recording Techniques 39

Setting Up Your First Base Line 41

Gridding a Site and Photo-Mosaics 47

Positioning Techniques to Grid a Site and Photo-Mosaics 49

Artifact Identification 55

Initial Artifact Handling 67

Underwater Excavation Techniques 73

Artifact Preservation Techniques 79

Long Term Artifact Stabilization Lab 83

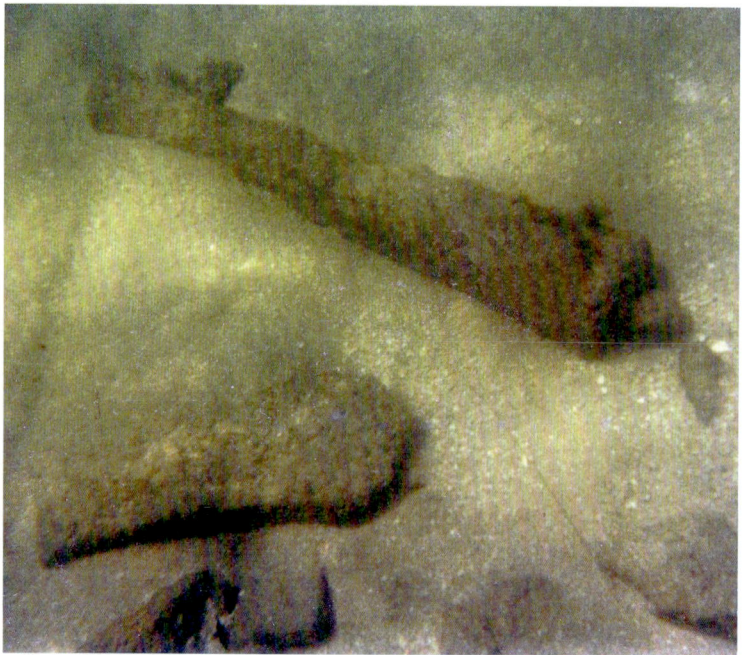

Cannons found on Jupiter Shipwreck Site
after prop-wash excavation

Introduction

Progressing SCUBA divers quickly begin to create niches of interest for themselves.

Typically, it is a shiny object or odd-shaped formation on the sea bottom that first grabs the attention of a snorkeler or diver, then stimulates his or her natural inquisitiveness. All the shipwreck tales we've heard since childhood and every movie we've ever seen about buccaneers and their treasure – from *Captain Blood* to *The Deep* to *Pirates of the Caribbean* – come rushing to mind; and subconsciously we ask: "Could this be sunken treasure?"

A significant step as one progresses in this wondrous adventure in discovery is to develop a better understanding of *underwater debris fields*. Both nature and man create "scatter patterns," and it is important to be able to recognize the differences among them. There are a number of varieties; and each may well be specific to the site you have come upon.

Some discoveries by SCUBA divers are caused of natural events that have occurred over millions of years. As discussed earlier, nature has its own methods of reclaiming its natural resources over time. Others of these sites are referred to within the anthropological community and now underwater archeological sub field, as either anomalies, "events" or "derived sites" – as they may turn out to be a mixture of debris dumped by man and natural disasters, such as earthquakes, land slides and tidal waves.

On the other hand, some are actually scatter patterns of lost, unknown or undocumented maritime events — known as *shipwreck* sites.

When one thinks of a shipwreck under the sea, popular nonfiction works like "Shadow Divers" and other publicized nautical events like the sinking and eventual re-discovery of the *Titanic* or the *Andrea Doria* conjure up shadowy images of either intact or major remains of denizens of the deep. These in fact do exist – in large numbers; but the shipwreck sites we are addressing in this work differ distinctly because the sea has, for the most part, reclaimed all but a few elusive clues and remnants of their former existence. It doesn't take long for the ravages of time and the sea to obscure the evidence of a hitherto lost maritime event.

Every week at least one or more vessels sink somewhere on our planet. Some of the events, over time, may earn historic status. Others simply become hazards to navigation and possibly a nuisance to maritime commerce. Still others will be lost in time. Since most of these events occur at or near shipping lanes, ships that have sunk are often blown up with explosives so that they will not pose a hazard to navigation. During the beginning of the age of discovery it was not uncommon for native peoples to torch or set fire to a near shore shipwreck site to prevent salvagers from finding the site and disrupting their daily routine. It is not unnatural that past or modern cultures may have dumped their own refuse atop many such sites – making them even more difficult to distinguish and classify.

"LOOK! DON'T TOUCH!" should not simply be a motto, but a *hard and fast rule* for most sport divers, especially for those new to venturing underwater. Natural coralline structures are very sensitive and in most cases should be just observed by us in their natural state. This is especially true if you are diving in a site unfamiliar to you. The natural inquisitiveness of the human spirit, however, makes that rule subject to a lot of liberal interpretation when a diver encounters an artifact or man-made item. Still, the motto — "LOOK! DON'T TOUCH!" — *should* hold fast for a very practical reason. You see, its "provenance" – that is to say, its point of discovery — may well be a determining factor in studying the entire "event" connected to how the item came to rest there.

The above axiom is not difficult to fathom in theory. Now enter the real world, and imagine you are snorkeling or SCUBA diving. An item catches your eye and it turns out to be a clump of encrusted silver coins, an emerald-encrusted 22 karat golden crucifix, or maybe an ornate bottle. Now, what do you do?

This does not only happen in movies like *The Deep* and *Into the Blue.* And when it happens in real life, looking and not touching seems to not make a whole lot of sense. The concept of "finders / keepers" is ingrained upon our brains as children, but does this now hold true? Suddenly, you will find yourself confronted with a whole new set of questions and moral dilemmas:

"Whose is this anyway?"
"What is it actually worth?"
"How did it get here?"

"Can I take it and maybe sell it?"

"If I leave it here, what if somebody else finds it and takes it?"

"Can I possibly find this spot again?"

"Do I even know exactly where I am?"

Depending upon your make up or nature, indoctrination, social consciousness and or common sense, you may choose to swim right past the item. On the other hand, the natural inquisitiveness that led you to be there in the first place more than likely will take over. The short and conservative approach is that you should mark the location, then check it out through local authorities and the local laws. Should you decide to take any action, remember that a level of responsibility goes along with the actions you are about to take. This book, using our practical experience of over two decades at the Jupiter Wreck Site attempts to outline the resources required and the initial steps for you to consider following prudently before you proceed.

17th century swivel cannon found by three firemen in a children's swim area in Jupiter, Florida. Irresponsibly they cut it into three pieces thinking that treasure was inside.

The first hard reality you have to quickly, yet maturely address is the who, what, when, where and why questions:

1. Is this just a unique recreational vacation dive for you in an area you may never return to?

2. Are you locally diving in an area close to home that is readily accessible to you?

3. Are there already known and documented sites within the area you are diving?

4. What are the risks and potential rewards of becoming more involved?

5. Are you really ready to undertake the tasks, risk and expense of becoming a participating responsible historic undersea explorer?

Before you answer "yes" to the latter question, you need to realize this may require a commitment of time and financial resources that may soon stretch far beyond your capabilities. It may put you at odds with local interests, specialized interest groups, local, provisional and national governments. What you do next may well be the biggest step you ever take into the unknown. At this point, it is entirely up to you. You may just decide to snap the object up, take it home and put it on your fireplace mantle, lock it up in a safe deposit box, bury it in the back yard or attempt to sell it!

At first the initial answers to these questions seemed easy for me.

When brought out to see where the first cannon and anchor were re-discovered in 1987 near the Jupiter Inlet on the southeast coast of Florida, I owned and operated a small marina, boat rental and marine service company in the area. Two local surfers spotted the first cannon and anchor, which were exposed by the shifting sands. They told a lifeguard who, at the time, was a good friend of mine. An employee recently had convinced me to become

PADI SCUBA certified. A local historical society was constructing a regional museum right down the street from my marina. At 39 years old, I was in reasonably good shape, had a lot of free time, nobody to answer to and was up for another adventure. Little did I know that the decisions I made in those first days of discovery were charting the course for the rest of my life.

Lucky for people living today in the 21st century, GPS positioning technology makes it relatively easy even for the least technical of us to have a pretty good idea where we are, even over water. Should you decide to become pro-actively involved, your first step should be to address the positioning question so you know where you first discovered the object that has captured your interest. I cannot begin to remember how many snorkelers and divers have come to me with stories of something they saw or found while diving. Three would-be treasure salvagers, in particular, come to mind. Each of these individuals came across what they were sure was an encrusted cannon just north of our wreck site at Coral Cove Park on Jupiter Island. The first two thought for sure they were only steps away from riches. They pondered for months about what to do. During the ensuing time, the shifting coastal sands covered it. When they finally came to me about it — well, they couldn't find it again! The problem is: *Where is it?*

Today's SCUBA divers have the ability to carry with them some basic communication equipment and non-destructive site marking tools. A dive slate and writing instrument is a good idea. An extra weight with an inflatable buoy and some line is ideal. Take an accurate visual fix with compass headings on your present area, notating the site location upon your dive slate. Note any visual points of interest, also with compass headings. No matter what your end game may be, not being able to return to the site is not a situation you want to be in. The third snorkeler who came across the alleged cannon, a trained land surveyor, took pains to take shore based reference points. When he brought me to the site he went right to the spot! There it was, between two major rock outcroppings – a well-encrusted acetylene bottle that probably rolled off a dredge or work boat years earlier!

The upcoming chapters will help you to develop the equipment package and basic skills to identify anomalies and unknown shipwreck sites, so as to better understand and thus protect what has come to be known as our "underwater historic cultural resources and heritage." It also will help you to systematically investigate a cultural site to better determine whether it is of a "derived nature" or is simply discarded material.

First and foremost, it is important for you to gain some practical knowledge of the areas you choose to dive.

If you are diving, just off Salt Island near Tortola, BritishVirgin Islands, and you happen across a shipwreck site, most likely it is the *RMS* (Royal Mail Steamship) *Rhone*. The *Rhone* is in a designated National Park. With all the tourists and recreational SCUBA divers that come to the Virgin Islands, sites such as the *Rhone* would be picked clean and destroyed if they were not protected. The same will hold true eventually for sites in more remote locations such as Truk Lagoon in the South Pacific where planes and ships that sank during World War II are designated as war graves and/or national historic cultural resources.

It won't take long for you to gain local knowledge of currently known sites. On the other hand, the shifting sands of fate and time, karma, good luck or bad, may confront you with a situation that is truly unique and hitherto unknown. How you choose to deal with it may determine much of your future.

My wife and I are documenting our experiences and our educational curve over the past two decades, so as to help you better comprehend some standards and parameters should you encounter anomalies or artifacts while free diving, snorkeling, hooka or SCUBA diving.

As you arrive at decision points while following the course of action you choose to follow, the complexity of the tasks at hand increases dramatically. Be ready for this and remember that I am warning you of the complexity of the adventure of discovery you are plunging yourself into. Keep in mind the example of the one answer to the question below:

"How can you pick out a true explorer standing within a group?"

Answer: "He is the one with all the arrows in his back! ...You see, he is so far out in front of everyone else, even his friends may be shooting at him. *Ouch!*"

The legal issues dealing with shipwrecks cannot be underestimated. You must attempt to abide by the law. The law is usually the single most important factor in determining if a project can move forward. For the sake of jurisprudence, let's assume you have yet to determine if this isolated find is part of a larger cultural resource or event.

Example of specialized undersea explorer equipment

Equipment Needs

To spend significant time underwater you obviously will need some sort of breathing air source and life support equipment such as Self Contained Underwater Breathing Apparatus, also known as SCUBA gear. A proper buoyancy compensation device (BCD), weight belt, mask, fins, snorkel and gloves will be a part of this package. Most important, however, you will need the proper training and certification, such as a PADI open-water diving course or, even better, participation in an Advanced Diver Certification Program.

Depending upon your dive site, the proper wet or dry diving suit is a must, as you will be spending more time under the water than the average recreational diver may be accustomed to. You should have with you a "dive buddy" or two who are equally as well trained and prepared; and you should have a extra person to serve as an "up" or "safety diver team tender."

In shallow water at a limited site, a hooka rig may be employed. "Hookas" are surface air breathing apparatuses that supply low pressure — 80 to 125 psi — breathing air via an oil-less air compressor, either powered by a combustion or electric engine. They got the name "hooka" because with two or more hoses running from a central contraption of sorts, they resemble a Turkish water pipe. But it is important to note that during the early stages of site identification, one rarely has any comprehension of the site's actual size. SCUBA allows you more freedom to search the initial parameters of your site.

Diver Tom Gidus holding an encrusted 17th Century Spanish Colonial coin while hooka diving on the Jupiter Wreck

You also will need two diver's slates with grease pencils, two or more marking floats, each with a good dive knife, various measuring devices, some stakes and small screw anchors (if there is a sand bottom), net bags and tags that can be used for marking descriptions or identifying numbers. A good underwater digital camera with digital time and date capabilities should be part of your gear. Your support diver should have a modern high quality portable or fixed-on-board GPS positioning system. If you don't already have one available, a pulse induction underwater metal detector also will be on your "want list." Luckily for us, we get a good amount of publicity from Trimble Navigation, which has a subsidiary called Tripod Data Systems, an organization that was kind enough to provide us with two hand-held Nomad Waterproof GPS units. These units have a touch screen, surface and underwater video/still cameras, are Bluetooth enabled and run a Windows Mobile platform. We show them being used at our shipwreck site on their Rugged Outdoors Web site.

Don't forget that all of your diving log books need to be with your group at all times, so notes can be taken by all parties and later compared.

Unless you are working from the shore line or beach, it is advisable to have a boat or, at the very least, an inflatable work platform or raft. It will allow you to carry, in an organized manner, all your gear.

As you may be noticing, what probably started out as a simple recreational dive is taking on a whole different dimension.

Remember:

Number 1:

If you put two or more people together in a situation like this, the confidentiality factor changes dramatically. (Why this is an important factor will be discussed later.)

Number 2:

The financial costs to assemble and support a three-member dive team and the equipment package I've described already surpass the cost of a half-decent used car. And, you really haven't gone back under the water yet.

Why?

Because before you splash in to undertake the initial recording and investigation of "*your* site" you need to create a sound dive plan that your team must follow and attempt to clearly and concisely document date, time, position, weather and sea conditions, participants and particulars of the dive.

If you are advanced divers, you probably already have the dive equipment at your disposal. If you are working in an area convenient to you, many of the items –such as line and measuring equipment — may be readily available. Today, many GSM cell phones have the GPS capabilities you can use to position yourself, *if* you are within a cell tower's range. If the location is near shore you can use an inexpensive electronic mapping device like a Tom Tom. For under $150.00 Delorme markets a GPS interface and positioning software you can hook up to a laptop. I have used this at the Jupiter Wreck site, as it is only 600 feet off the beach.

If you don't have a wad of cash or an expensive research vessel at your disposal, don't give up. Many accomplished explorers and salvagers over the past 400 years have been quite successful working from the beach. For instance, Dan Porter, a successful undersea explorer near Sebastian, Florida, used an old 16-foot Hobie Cat without a mast as his equipment and undersea exploration platform and discovered hundreds of thousands of dollars worth of lost 18th century treasures.

What is most important, at this juncture, is for you to develop your systematic observational technique and some good common sense to help control the endorphins, adrenalin and pure, old-fashioned excitement your new undersea adventures will be generating.

33

At this point, let's review the specifics of our exploration scenario. …

You were on a recreational dive in an area that is readily accessible to you. You came across an interesting anomaly, an artifact or article fashioned or used by man. The item, in your opinion, is significant enough to demand further study. You have reasoned it should be removed from its location based upon your concern that its perceived value – if encountered by someone not as trustworthy and honorable as you – might cause that person to take it from its surroundings without responsibly recording its initial location, thus eliminating it as a potential meaningful clue to what might be a significantly larger event.

You fully realize that at this point you may be operating outside of the local laws and possibly subject to arrest and forfeiture of your equipment and vessel, but you decide to act anyway. Be aware you are now faced with a practical and moral dilemma. You may be viewed by others as a pirate, scoundrel or, even worse, a thief.

You have marked the spot, recorded its location well enough that you have been able to easily return to it with your team, and you have the basic tools necessary to properly observe the potential of whether this artifact location is just an isolated incident or part of a larger picture. You have developed a dive plan so that your team can make a more responsible observation of the immediate area surrounding your initial find to see if there may be related items. You have made sufficient local inquires if this may be a previously discovered or known underwater site or event, so that you are not maliciously about to break any laws that may put your team, equipment and you at risk.

Another important tool for you to acquire at this juncture is an underwater metal detector. From my experience, a reliable and well-built pulse induction metal detector is best. I suggest that you procure more than one unit because these are sensitive battery operated electronic devices. They are being used in a harsh environment and are subject to mis-calibration and malfunction in the field. Although you may have first encountered an artifact upon the sea bed surface - the presence of a functional pulse induction metal detector may lead to other artifacts that have scoured themselves beneath the sea bed surface.

Using a metal detector under water is a skill that is easy to develop. By taking certain objects in a controlled area and burying them under the sand or rocks, you can then test the operational characteristics and sensitivity of your particular device and hone your under water detection skills.

Remember, in the open ocean and along the shore a current can easily sweep away your metal detector if and when you set it aside to excavate an anomaly or metal hit. It is always better to have it somehow tethered or attached to you. The detection envelop of these units vary dependent upon their circuitry and detection loop size. The size, material make up, and mass are also factors. For instance, an iron cannon may be detected with four to six or more feet of sand or overburden. A silver coin the size of a silver dollar may give a signal up to 18 inches beneath overburden to a well tuned pulse induction metal detector. Gold pieces of jewelry have a slighter detection envelop.

Depending upon the human traffic over your search area, prepare yourself for discovering countless lead weights, beer cans, fishing lures, nuts and bolts, old spikes, outboard motor parts and other items that you may find less interesting than whatever you came to search for.

At the Jupiter Shipwreck site we have spent hours excavating, on occasion, to find at the bottom of a hole: street no parking signs and auto wheel parking lot concrete bumpers with iron rod reinforcement. These came from earlier parking lots constructed in the park on reclaimed beach from past public works dredging projects. Tropical storm events had washed the parking lots away and thus on top of our 17th century shipwreck site. Nevertheless, you remove the item if it is a high energy surf zone situation. Why? Because if you go back to that area at a later date, you don't want to spend hours again – re-finding an old no parking sign!

Site Recording Techniques

It is important to note that many significant facts are lost in time. Taking the time to write down the circumstances of an event within a logical framework is an important step so that others may become aware of your discovery and analyze its significance.

The State of Florida's Division of Historical Resources has come up with a proven, acceptable system of maintaining notes for underwater recording of "field work." Aside from your divers slates and grease pencils, it is best to get used to using an acceptable standardized format of recording site data, even outside of the state's waters. When and if professional public employees evaluate your data at a later date, they will be less likely to discount your work if it is recorded in a format approved by and thus familiar to them. (Attached is the Florida form. It is usually filled in, in triplicate. We have committed ours to a computer format for easier use.)

FLORIDA DEPARTMENT OF STATE · BUREAU OF ARCHAEOLOGICAL RESEARCH
DAILY FIELD NOTE AND ACTIVITY LOG · FOR DGPS POSITION FINDING

Permit # _____ Date _____ SubC No. _____ FMSF # and Wreck _____ Page _____ of _____

Summary of Activities _____

Captain _____ Crew _____ Weather and Sea State _____ Work Vessel _____

Archaeologist _____ Data Recorder _____

Work Time Hrs. _____ Comments _____

Archaeological Field Notes and Materials Recovered and/or Located

Unit/ Anomaly #	Lat.	Decimal	Lon.	Decimal	Bottom Terrain Overburden Depth Water Visibility	Depth	Tag Number	Qty.	Description

This is to certify that this information is true and correct.

Date: _____ Signatures: _____ Captain _____ Archaeologist _____

HRI6E067 Rev. 06/08 Rule 1A-31.060(11), F.A.C.

Florida Department of State - Bureau of Archeological
Research Daily Field Note and Activity Log -
For DGPS Position Finding

Setting Up Your First Base Line

To begin with, be aware that it is impossible to immediately discern the size and overall scope of a specific individual underwater archeological site from the position of your first isolated find.

The Original Jupiter Primary Site

Archeological stratification or the "Layering Theory," developed over the last 200 years by professional land-based and university-trained geological and archeological students, most likely will not apply in the near-shore underwater environment where you may have made your initial find. Still, you now need to formulate a plan to assemble a "window" of observation that is manageable for your initial capabilities. Land-based anthropologists who specialize in the field of study of archeology and professional underwater archeology follow basically the same procedure.

The first step is to establish a manageable "base line." The base line consists of two points within the site-specific area from which you may construct a reproducible diagram of your exploration dive plan that you can later study, refer to and to which you can add newly discovered data.

In the case of the 1987 Jupiter Shipwreck Site, it did not take us more than four dives in 10 to 13 feet of "gin clear water" just south of the present day inlet to locate three more cannons from the initial find of the first cannon and anchor. We then set up a 75-foot base line starting north of cannon #1 to just south of cannon #4. It is important to note that this base line needs to be as permanently affixed as possible since all of the measurements

that follow will be related to it. We used 4-foot long screw anchors.
These can be purchased at most hardware stores.

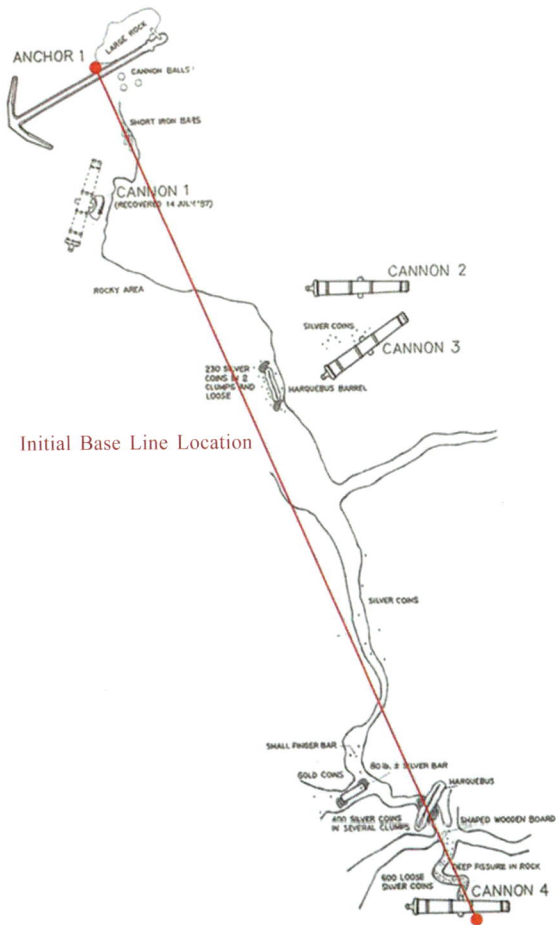

Base Line Drawing

The base line starting point was just 5 feet north of the first anchor located on a centerline and the ending point was located about 5 feet south of cannon #4. The screw anchors were first used and a line marked with 1-foot intervals was strung between the two points. From such a procedure base line measurements can be taken, allowing the team to form a grid of and location position for other possible finds related to the event you are now responsibly documenting. In the case of our initial Jupiter Site, significant numbers of other related artifacts soon were located and a picture began to form opening a window to the past.

This is relatively straight forward and not rocket science if you have decided to continue.

Using a non-stretchable measuring tape or datum rod (segmented in inches or centimeters) consistent with your original base line, measure the distance from the closest base line point, noting the item's original location and compass headings in relation to the measuring point, at right angles along the base line.

If the artifacts you are encountering are abundant, you may choose to assemble a measuring "sub grid" using weighted PVC pipe with holes drilled into it so that buoyant air can escape as you take it underwater. Many underwater explorers use such grids with a fixed centered camera attachment so they can assemble a photo-mosaic grid.

Every underwater cultural resource site will have its own unique characteristics. In the case of our Jupiter Shipwreck Site there was an abundance of artifacts that could immediately be specifically dated and identified – Spanish Colonial coins, or *pieces of eight, with dates actually stamped upon them!*

These coins were made of silver, irregularly shaped, about the size of an early U.S. silver dollar. The initial find of coins were coated with either a brown or black concretion of marine life mixed with silver sulfite, masking their specific identifying characteristics. Still, there was no question that they were coins. It took a hammer and chisel to break the first of them loose from the surfaces to which time and the elements had connected them.

Cleaned Spanish Colonial Coins

recovered off the Jupiter Shipwreck

One may argue that if you had to break them away with a chisel, then they probably were safe there "in situ" – that is to say, in the position and place where they had come to rest. However, upon further observation we were able to locate "burn marks" on surrounding bottom locations where other artifacts had laid. These artifacts had been removed—we only can assume—by less enlightened or less historically responsible individuals who happened to come across them. Thus, it did not take long for us to realize that the "timeless time capsule" argument some within the archeological community use when describing underwater shipwreck sites does not always hold water, particularly in the surf zone. In the real world — especially in high energy surf zones or locations easily accessible through modern technology – the capsule is more than a little vulnerable.

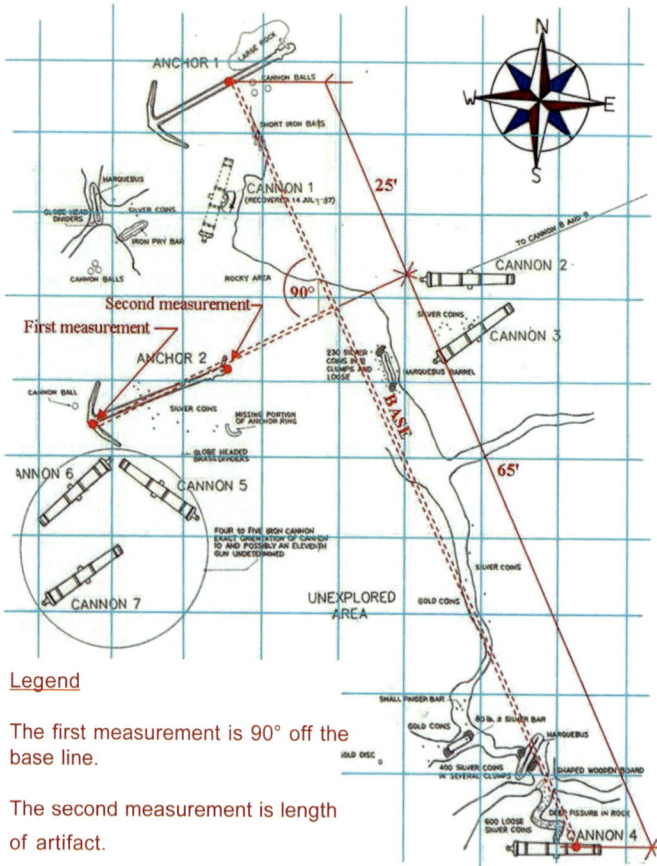

Legend

The first measurement is 90° off the base line.

The second measurement is length of artifact.

This grid resembles the upper deck of a ship.

All cannons were found upside down.

Positioning Techniques to Grid a Site and Photo-Mosaics

At the Jupiter Shipwreck Site, we did not set up a photo-mosaic grid. Honestly, we didn't know any better. More time was spent with lifeguards taking pictures of each other posing by the cannons, anchors and other concreted scattered artifacts. Conditions could have been ideal for a photo mosaic, but in 1987 digital underwater photography and underwater camera housings for sport divers had yet to come onto the market. Today — depending on your budget, the visibility at your site and presence of overburden – sand—it can be a good idea to have multiple cameras running continuous video whenever you are working at the site to document your methods and actions.

To set up a basic photo mosaic grid in less than 50 feet of clear water with reasonable visibility, a two-yard, or meter, PVC tripod grid arrangement works well. But if your work platform is not big enough to accommodate this equipment on deck, scaling the size down to one yard or meter will do. In terms of the tripod, think of a pyramid with equilateral legs.

As for cameras, digital definitely is the way to go. Canon Digital Cameras offer many underwater housing units designed for its specific models and brands of digital cameras. With digital storage capabilities as they now are you can store and process the hundreds of photographs a reasonably well-assembled photo-mosaic will require.

By the way, leaving the camera down there is not a good idea. It most likely will become another artifact some other diver absconds with! Take it with you after each dive. Unless you're independently wealthy, forget about using film. It's just too cost prohibitive.

The sub-grid system is being used in the following photo outside of the water to illustrate an assortment of ballast stones recovered from the Jupiter Shipwreck site. Its use underwater comes in handy when one is attempting to document the location of multiple small items that may be uncovered and/or recovered along the initial base line.

Early Jupiter Wreck Ballast Rocks

The above PVC grid is sectioned off into 6-inch alternating white and red segments and is 3 feet square. (Note: You may prefer to use the metric system, but whichever methodology you choose, stick with it and note it on your field notes.)

Vessels other than dugout canoes can be made up of many items. So, when a vessel has met its end, the "scattered remains" of it left on the bottom often can be used to help tell the story of the events leading to the vessel's demise. If you have come across a primary site, there may be many items present; therefore, a single combined photo mosaic base-line drawing may eventually become a blur, and different smaller scale photo mosaics and individual drawings may be required to maintain understandable detail.

Summary of Setting Up a Photo Mosaic

Photo mosaic graphing and video of a site with 21st century technology is extremely helpful, but a human drawing of a site often reveals more of a site's discerning characteristics. It's important to note that the scatter pattern of a site is often masked by "overburden" — be it sand, silt, rock, dumped modern debris and even other shipwreck material or remains. Photo mosaics and video do not factor this out. A drawing can.

By creating an acceptable sub grid of PVC and adding triangular upright legs to hold the camera at the proper predetermined angle, multiple still or video images can be taken, and later reproduced and assembled to form a photo mosaic of your site.

Some of you may notice at this point what started out as a new adventure is now taking on a life of its own - resembling a job!

Others will view their inquisitive efforts as the satisfaction of a growing passion, similar to your discovery of sex.

Captain Dom pointing to
formation of concreted boulders

Artifact Identification

The definition of an artifact is an item that is used or made by man. What they may look like after being immersed underwater and how to identify them need to be discussed together.

I have observed divers frantically digging a hole so hard that they were scooping artifacts away without recognizing them - only to get to the bottom of the hole.

The hard bottom of your particular site — visible once sand or overburden has been removed, either naturally or unnaturally — may have natural geological cracks and/or striations created over the millennia. In the case of the Jupiter Site, we often encountered piles of boulders. Artifacts eventually settle into the cracks between the boulders and concrete together.

As you delve deeper into the responsible study and documentation of what may be a maritime event, more and more encrusted objects – or E.O.s – likely will be discovered. If you don't have a sound plan in place to record their initial provenance and journey through what may be an extended identification and restoration process, it doesn't take long for them to get mixed up.

Man-made items constructed from metal or wood rapidly deteriorate in a marine environment. They often become encrusted or concreted together and, to the naked eye, are indiscernible. Here is where a metal detector becomes helpful, but don't become over reliant on it. Your observational skills – *your eyes!* — are your best tools. Better spherical vision was one of man's pre-archaic survival mechanisms. This likely will become more exercised and thus finely tuned in an underwater environment. Learn to refine and use this ancient survival tool.

If you have made it this far, you and your team are literally and figuratively totally immersed in this effort. More than likely the word has spread of your work. Why? Because it is natural to want to share and even embellish the adventures in discovery your team is experiencing. Once there are two or more people involved, there is no such thing as a secret and if there are any valuables involved, here is where your problems will become amplified.

Spotting E.O.s

An E.O. or encrusted object

To some, encrusted objects – sometimes known as "clumps" or E.O.s – may initially resemble a concreted cow patty. Weight of the E.O. can be a dead give-a-way as to its contents. An Encrusted Object (E.O.) with more "mass" or weight will cause itself to sink deeper into natural surrounding sediments.

Upon closer observation, please note (above) the distinct round, flat shapes stacked along the bottom lower edge and leading up the right side. Also note the green tint leaching out from areas on the encrustation. This almost always indicates the presence of copper or brass, but in this E.O. it is copper alloy leaching out of the silver encrusted coins. In this case, you don't have to have a metal detector to figure out there is something in this encrustation deserving of further study.

In the case of the above E.O., it contained over 80 coins.

Most E.O.s you encounter won't be filled with Spanish colonial coins. They may contain a mixture of both ferrous and non-ferrous decomposing metal and organic materials, broken pottery shard or glass fragments, cannon balls, spark plugs, nuts and bolts, or what have you. The only way to find out what is inside an E.O. is to carefully clean the object. However, there is a significant protocol to follow *before* one starts any cleaning and artifact identification and preservation process.

Your first step upon discovering the object is to photograph it where you first saw it. Using your underwater digital camera with a time and date function, make sure to have both the camera and this function turned on and correct. Superimpose the time and date on the photos. Doing so will help you connect your photo record with your field notes.

Also, if at all possible, include in each photo frame a standardized identifiable measuring device, such as a ruler or L-square ruler.

The next step is to assign a unique coded number and clearly describe the E.O.'s location in your field notes. It is critical for you to specify when and where the E.O. was found along the base line and affix a plastic tag to the E.O. Stainless steel tie wire is good for this purpose.

Two E.O.s containing similar items;
one partially cleaned

Are shipwrecks really "Timeless Time Capsules"?

Shipwrecks are catastrophic events. Seldom are the remains of such events lying on the bottom intact. However, many misinformed "experts" insist on a theory that basically states: "All Shipwrecks Are Timeless Time Capsules." Frankly, such talk only serves to mislead the unenlightened. It is not an accurate statement or description of most shipwreck events, as they deteriorate over time - plain and simple.

People of the past may not have had the advantage of today's technology, but they were not stupid, and their motivations were, pretty much, similar to our own. Survival tops the list of basic motivations, with sustenance and greed tied for a close second. Immediately after a sinking or shipwreck, once one's survival seems secure, the concept of recovery of whatever one can salvage quickly enters one's thoughts.

I've experienced this first hand, having lost a vessel in a storm in the Bahamas. I actually was calling in MAYDAYS on a cell phone as the vessel went under the water. I popped up with the cell phone still stuck to my ear, took a look at it, flipped it over my shoulder and began to swim for my life, using a plastic gas can as a flotation device.

Luckily for my crew, two strap-hanging passengers (people who are just along for the ride) and myself, I had raised the dock master on a neighboring island and he sent two fishermen out to rescue us from a nearby rock atoll.

When I called the owner of the vessel, I told him, "I've got some good news and some bad news. The good news is we are all alive. The bad news is *The Hydrosweep* just sank and is sitting on the bottom on the edge of the Bahama Banks. If we don't get her raised ASAP, we are going to have an environmental catastrophe."

I was given a blank check, and within a week I had the *MRV Hydrosweep* disassembled, up on the deck of an inter-island freighter with all her fuel and hydraulic fluids still in her tanks, and on the way back to the mainland.

To my knowledge, today's telling of the story is the only "archeological record" of that event, recorded and thus shared in the public domain. This is just one example that not every story gets to be told. And as the rule – more than the exception to the rule – the story is usually subjective and subject to the storyteller's interpretation. There is no physical record of this shipwreck event remaining on the bottom for future generations to study.

So much for the "timeless time capsule" idea.

A shipwreck scatter pattern may be made up of multiple debris fields. Depending upon where you are diving, the rate of deterioration and encrustation most likely has masked or made the immediate complete identification of the objects almost impossible.

A basic rule to remember is: The law of gravity is the single most important factor in evaluating whether this is a shipwreck site or just a partial and isolated scatter or represents cargo having been dumped over the side. This was often done to lighten a load if a vessel was approaching a shoal area. There may be no shipwreck to find.

Unlike most land sites, the stratification or layering of overburden covering artifacts underwater, especially in the sea, is highly subject to wind, wave action and tidal currents, along with a host of other factors. As organic material deteriorates, the mass or weight of metal objects has a tendency to cause artifacts to settle deeper or scour themselves into the ever-changing sub-surface stratum of the seabed. It is important to note here that the heaviest objects have a tendency to settle the deepest until they reach bedrock or an obstruction — like boulders or even another artifact, which might be totally unrelated to the event you are studying.

Shipwreck Related Artifacts
(cannon balls, ship's knee, arquebus barrel & hammer)

Once you have documented the E.O.'s position and determined it should be removed for further study, evaluation and preservation, and you are capable of bringing it to the surface safely, it should be rinsed with fresh water as soon as possible, retagged, if necessary, bagged and placed in a well-marked and sturdy container filled with fresh water. If fresh water is not available, use salt water; but, whatever you do, keep the artifact underwater.

Remember, the "deterioration clock" immediately speeds up the moment the E.O. hits the atmosphere.

If you are, in fact, exploring a hitherto unrecorded maritime loss, artifacts and E.O.s both related to and unrelated are quickly going to begin to add up. Their proper documentation, safe storage, preservation and final disposition will make the difference as to whether you are branded a "scoundrel" by some or applauded by others who see you as a responsible undersea explorer adding to the public's knowledge of our maritime past. No matter how superbly you do the job, be prepared for some eggs to be thrown your way. The "scoundrel" tag likely will be placed on you by many overzealous university-trained archeologists more interested in control of the permitting process than the ultimate knowledge these events contain.

Yvonne Addario recovering an encrusted coin after hand-fanning technique

Initial Artifact Handling

It is important to understand at this juncture that you are undertaking a *major* task. Many professional anthropologists and archeologists view the sport diver as they would a well-meaning tourist who may have found a baby alligator, exotic snake or purchased a potbelly piglet. Sure, such creatures initially are cute or intriguing, but as they grow they can become major problems. The bewildered owner often finds himself or herself looking for a place to get rid of the unwanted "object."

In the same way, it doesn't take long for the assemblage of artifacts and E.O.s from a shipwreck or emerging scatter pattern to overwhelm the average, even well-meaning and responsible undersea explorer. An example of this problem can be gleaned from our experience with fish weights at the Jupiter Shipwreck Site.

When I first started finding fish weights unrelated to our shipwreck event, I hooked them to a pith helmet I wore when top side. At first it looked cute, but soon the pith helmet became deformed from the weight of the ever-increasing number of fishing weights. Next, I decided to cull the modern fish weights from the older ones and threw the others into a 5-gallon pail. Soon, the pail began to fill up. That's how it goes when you start exploring and salvaging from most debris fields.

It is important to note here that if it is metal and non-event related, go ahead and bring it up anyway, if at all possible. Otherwise, you may be spending hours re-finding it at a later date.

In any case, whatever you are finding and have decided to recover and preserve may soon outstrip your capabilities for storage and stabilization. You might think you can pass the material on to the public sector. Think again. Even if there is a historical agency or society in your area, it is highly unlikely the institution will have the budget, facilities, professional staff or additional space to help with the daunting task you have unilaterally decided to undertake. That is one of the main reasons why the "look don't touch" philosophy has gained legitimacy and is the standard recommended by the publicly employed archeological community.

Therefore we must return to our original premises concerning (a) what should be removed from a site; (b) the importance of original site documentation; and (c) follow through during the preservation processes – all of which becomes *your* primary responsibility if you truly are a responsible undersea explorer.

The storage, preservation and cleaning of artifacts is an arduous process. A sufficient, secure and yet well-ventilated area with a readily available fresh water supply, electricity, security and tool storage is needed.

Such work also can be quite dirty and create noxious odors and unsafe gases.

When an E.O. is broken open, decomposing ferrous metals – some hundreds of years old — often smell like rotten eggs. Hydrogen sulfide gases can be a by-product of running artifacts through electrostatic reduction tanks; and solutions need to be regularly changed. The use of caustic soda amplifies the danger and risks. Plus, the black, grainy remains of decomposing metal leaves whatever it touches with a stubborn stain. Gloves most certainly are required for handling items.

An Artifact Laboratory Log is the first and foremost necessity. (A computer can be used for this purpose, but *be sure to back up all entries*.) Many of the entries that were on your field notes – possibly a copy of them as well — should be attached or referenced with each entry or item you and your team now have in your custody and care.

Heavy industrial-type plastic containers of varying sizes with sealable lids make good long-term artifact containers.

Depending on the number of E.O.s and their composition, a series of shelves to hold the containers – or, better yet, a more permanent and consistent container storage system—should be implemented that can address present and future preservation techniques and needs.

Whatever your storage method, *never forget*: The tagging process must follow the E.O.s and artifacts so that each item's original provenance is maintained.

Larger E.O.s containing possibly multiple items may well require a sub-numbering system as they go through the separation, cleaning and preservation processes. Don't be surprised to sometimes encounter unrelated items in an E.O. As anomalies constantly are being moved about – in most cases causing objects to deteriorate — the specific mass of such objects has a tendency to have them seeking their lowest attainable level or stratum. In a near-shore environment, sediments can come and go, and are moving about at a rapid rate. Those sediments can move artifacts long distances. Over the millennia, moving water has carved mountain ranges with glacial movement and created terrestrial wonders, such as the Grand Canyon. Currents resulting from moving water flow—based on the dictum of the "incompressibility of Water"—can shuffle objects about on the ever shifting seabed. The result may be that a spark plug thrown over one's shoulder while working on a modern outboard motor may be found next to a Spanish colonial coin minted 350 years ago.

Lakes, rivers, ocean shorelines and seabeds have a pulse and movement has a rhythm all its own. This rhythm beats to a different clock than we use on the surface.

This photo illustrates the Jupiter Shipwreck

Anchor Site after prop-wash excavation

Underwater Excavation Techniques

An understanding of this can start with mastering the art of "hand fanning". Just by gently waving your hand back and forth under water, you can move sediments to better make observations. Legendary undersea explorer, Teddy Tucker taught me how to use a ping pong paddle to accelerate this method of excavation. You must remember that ping pong paddles are made of wood and, if you let go, will certainly float away if you don't have them secured in some manner.

Use of any other mechanical means for excavation discussed in this chapter may be in violation of local laws. It is your responsibility to research this.

It is important for you to develop a basic understanding of hydro-dynamics. Speaking of which — as water cannot be compressed, it can be used as a medium to move material, sand and other types of overburden directionally to enhance one's ability to better study a shipwreck. For example, in 1987 we used the "Venturi Effect" of accelerating the speed of a liquid flow to uncover the tops of the first cannons and anchor at the Jupiter Shipwreck Site. We accomplished this by placing rocks in a pile upstream of the tidal current flow.

An example of the Venturi Effect in nature is the increase of tidal current and/or wave action as it approaches shallow water near shore. Undersea explorers or treasure hunters are forever attempting to come up with innovative ways of channeling available energy to excavate deeper into the substratum. For example, an underwater weir can be set up with a pile of rocks upstream of an area that is subject to significant current or tidal flow, thus directing the force of the tidal current to scour sand and overburden away from an area one wishes to investigate.

Deflectors and/or other prop wash devices — often called "mail boxes" — are used to rapidly move sand, sludge, mud or overburden. They also can be used to transport "clean water" to a site, depending upon the turbidity present at the depth where the team is working.

The negative impact of this type of excavation is: the deeper one has to excavate, the larger the column of water must be. Also, the column of water indiscriminately moves everything in its path that is not firmly concreted to the hard bottom. Large mailboxes or "blowers" can blow right through an ancient and deteriorating shipwreck site, dispersing artifacts over an even larger area. I am not suggesting they not be used; but I am saying they have their limitations and the potential for negative impacts, and thus should be used with care.

Traditional Twin Blowers

Another problem with prop-wash devices, either mailboxes or deflectors, is that they can theoretically dig a hole only so deep without creating a large berm or ridge around the upper edge of the hole. The ridge can become so large that new sand or overburden cannot be lifted over it. At that point, if you are not yet reaching "hard bottom," all you are doing is either driving artifacts that have more specific "mass" than the sand deeper still into the stratum; or you're simply moving the artifacts around the hole! By the time divers return to the hole, so much sand has fallen back into it the only artifacts still around will be located about a third to half way up the hole – where it has either been blown or remained, as yet undisturbed.

Deflectors attached to the *MRV Enterprise*

At the Jupiter Shipwreck Site, the maximum depth of a hole with blowers or set of Mailboxes (see photos) has been about a maximum of 32 feet from the water's surface in a static depth (before excavating of 10 to 14 feet given tidal height).

A more efficient, though slower and more costly methodology, is to use a hydro lift, airlift or venturie type dredge with trained observation divers close at hand.

Once you are digging past a depth deeper than 10 to 15 feet, air also can be injected into the high-pressure stream of water, enhancing the hydrolift's capability. At more than (33 feet), air alone can operate an efficient device known as an "airlift." However, in shallow water, the size of a compressor needed to run an airlift is prohibitive.

When thinking of a hydro-lift, think of a swimming pool vacuum. For the airlift, just think of the bubbles in champagne or soda pop. In a tube, as the air rises to the surface, it creates suction.

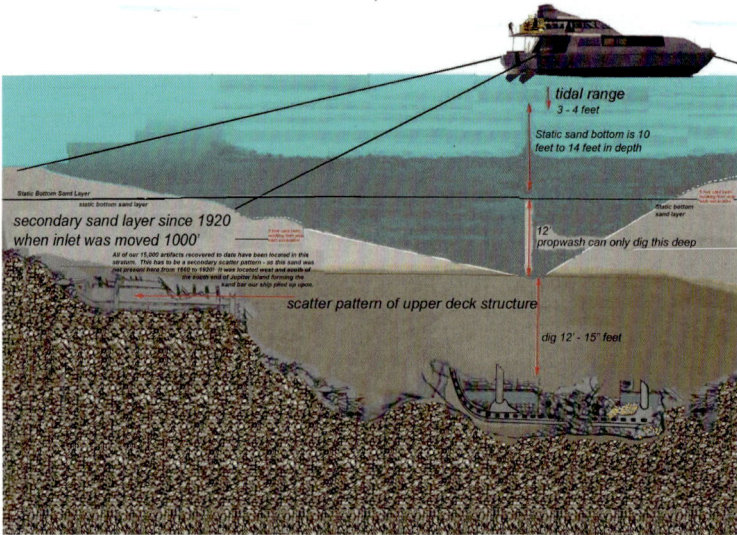

Cross Sectional Illustration of ratio of depth to hole

Artifact Preservation Techniques

Various investigation tools, ranging from dentists' elements, tooth brushes, jewelers tools to sledge hammers and chisels – depending upon the size and scope of your recovered E.O. s will be needed. Digital scanning and photographing equipment, solid work benches, work sink basins, sufficient exhaust fans, if working inside, long term storage soaking tanks are the first items on your list to acquire. Certain chemicals are also used in the preservation processes of various artifacts.

This can be a dangerous process and harmful to an observers health. Dangerous gases like hydrogen sulfide can be produced by electrostatic reduction that we will briefly discuss on our next section. Dangerous gases like hydrogen sulfide must not be inhaled, breathed and or be exposed to for a prolonged period without the use of a respirator.

Now, we've already established that when first encountered artifacts often are concreted together in clumps, or E.O.s. These E.O.s can be small or massive, and can look to the untrained eye like a natural feature of the seabed. (Note: A metal detector often is the best way for a novice explorer to tell the difference between a natural formation and an encrusted object, (E.O.) possibly containing artifacts

Once you have discovered what you believe to be an E.O. and have brought it to the surface, it is *imperative* that you remember, encrusted objects be kept re-immersed or stored in water once more – preferably fresh water.

Doing so is important because over time microscopic salt crystals seep into the grain of metal and wooden objects in the sea. If an artifact simply is mechanically cleaned by having its encrustations removed and then left to dry out, the salt crystals expand between the grain or substructure of the item and the artifact begins to come apart.

Cannon Ball cleaned and not properly conserved

We've also established that an E.O. may contain unrelated material to a specific event you are investigating. So, to properly study an E.O., the contents must be mechanically separated and then the items must be stabilized and preserved.

Divers hand-fan sand out from crack
in hard rock bottom.

Long Term Artifact Stabilization Lab

Equipment Needs of a long Term Artifact Storage and Preservation Lab Area are substantial.

Digital scanning and photographing equipment, solid work benches, work sink basins, sufficient exhaust fans (if working inside), long-term storage/soaking tanks are the first items on your list to acquire. Various investigative tools — ranging from chisels and sledge hammers to dentists' picks and probes and tooth brushes to jewelers tools – will be required depending on the size and scope of your recovered E.O.

A poly organic acidic chemical formulated to attack calcium carbonate formations but not metals can be used to expedite the removal of encrusted material. (Note: One such commercial chemical is Aracon, a poly organic acid similar to a pipe descaling solution which softens the encrustations with minimal damage to metal surfaces.)

Different methodology for preservation depends on the make up of the item you are attempting to preserve. There are a number of professional treatise and well-written books on the subject. So as to do preservation justice, I suggest further research be made.

Other chemicals also are used in the preservation processes of various artifacts. This can be quite dangerous. For instance, the chemicals used in the electrolytic reduction process produce dangerous gases, including hydrogen sulfide. Such gases cannot be tolerated for long without a respirator.

However, if you are going to clean and preserve an artifact, an effort must be made to drive salt crystals from the interior of the object; and electrolytic reduction – also known as electrostatic reduction — is a methodology often utilized to stabilize the effects of electro-galvanic corrosion. Such corrosion occurs over time when two or more dissimilar metals are immersed in salt water.

In electrolytic reduction, an electrolyte solution of soda ash with the ratio of 48:1 (water to any of the three electrolytes: salt, lemon juice or soda ash) can be used to stabilize silver, brass, bronze and copper artifacts with a minor negative current controlled by a voltage controlling device. One such unit is called a Variac 110 AC voltage control regulator. A power supply similar to one used for plating metals will also work. Attach such a unit to a 12 volt – 3 amp power supply. The use of the voltage control device is important because it can effectively step down the voltage and amperage to acceptable levels so as to not "cook" the coins.

A mild negative current is run through the coins and a positive charge is run through a stainless steel bolt into the solution. Note: *Only* stainless steel clips and anodes are to be used. When I first started "running" coins, I made the mistake of using alligator clips that were made of copper and only chrome plated. I then compounded my error by "pushing," or raising the amperage by increasing the voltage with the Variac. We ended up calling that batch of cleaned coins our "Izod Coins". The raised amperage actually pushed some of the copper from the inferior alligator clips into the coin specimens, making them look like they were bitten by a small alligator you see on Izod sports shirts!

When the coins are removed from the electrolytic solution, they are soaked in a mixture of baking soda and water. The mixture of baking soda solution is not critical. It is used to neutralize any corrosive moistness from this preservation process. The artifact, or in this case coin, is then rubbed with dried baking soda to remove the blackened and loosened encrustations, then placed back in their respective numbered bags.

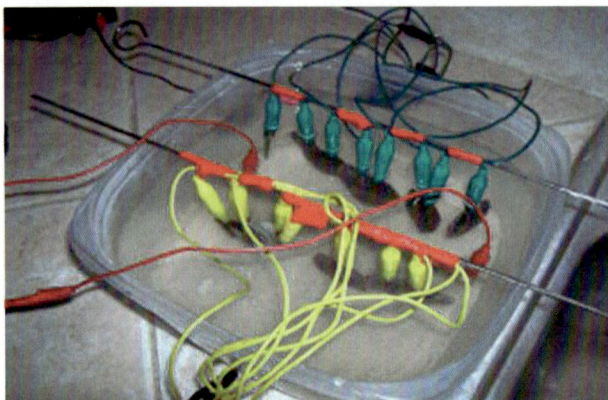

Electrolytic Reduction of Coins

During this preservation process it is easy to mix up the bagged artifact specimen numbers from the artifacts going through the cleaning and preservation process. Maintaining a proper artifact preservation log helps to eliminate or at least reduce the opportunity for this to occur. If in the process of cleaning an E.O. more individual artifacts begin to present themselves - one must list this in the artifact preservation log and create a secondary numbering system to document the additional knowledge and finds.

SUMMARY

Being a generalist who, for better or worse, has "been there…. and, done that," I have done my best here to briefly touch upon what I would call "decision points" that any responsible individual should consider as they take the plunge – literally and figuratively into undersea exploration. Adventure can become intoxicating and one must be careful not to have that "rush" lead one into danger – the progression of which can be multiplied ten-fold underwater.

Consider that a major commitment to the exploration of an undersea event can lead to an overextension or exhaustion of your physical, personal and financial resources. Weigh carefully that a welcome break in your routine to enjoy a treasure-hunting adventure can result in long-term negative consequences for the quality of life of those around you. You may suddenly find yourself in violation of the law and be labeled a scoundrel or even worse - *pirate!* Do not take this lightly and assume this book is instructing you to move forward in spite of the law. Dedication to such a project can lead to obsession and interfere with whatever it is you do to make a living — to feed your family and pay your bills. It also is important to note that not every past event needs to be studied and documented. My personal opinion is that the study of a past event is superfluous if it cannot benefit both the present and future. However, I'm not always right.

This treatise purpose is to act as a guide and attempt to inform you as to some of the responsibilities you should consider as you embark on whatever course of action you may choose to chart for yourself. There are a number of old adages out there that may apply to a newly committed, responsible undersea explorer. Let me leave you with but a few of them:

"If it was easy, everyone would be doing it".

"If you are going to take the front of the line, expect to get some eggs thrown at you".

"A journey of a thousand miles begins with a single step. And finally … Going to sea and just staying on the top of it is like going to the circus and staying outside of the tent!"

Good luck, my friends.
God's speed, and dive safe.

Captain Dom

For those Master Divers or Educational Instructing Institutes wishing to teach a PADI approved Distinctive Specialty Diver Training Course, questions and answer pamphlets are available at www.jupitercoins.com.